WAR MANUAL

A Field Guide for Soldiers in Christ
(Past and Present Warfare)

By Laura Kestly

ISBN: 978-1-78364-469-8

THE OPEN BIBLE TRUST
Fordland Mount, Upper Basildon,
Reading, RG8 8LU, UK.

www.obt.org.uk

> *"For though we walk in the flesh,*
> *we do not war after the flesh:*
> (For the weapons of our warfare are not carnal,
> but mighty through God to the pulling down of strongholds;)
> Casting down imaginations,
> and every high thing that exalts itself against the knowledge of God,
> and bringing into captivity every thought to the obedience of Christ."

War Manual

Contents

Page

5   The Great War: The Conflict Begins

11   Getting to Know the Enemy

15   History and Prophecy of the Enemy

21   Past Warfare: Historical Records

45   The Parable of the Weeds (Tares)

51   Present Warfare

69   Epilogue: Satan, the Enemy, is a Defeated Foe!

73   Terms to Know

77   More on Satan

80   About the Author

81   Free Sample

83   About this Book

THE GREAT WAR: THE CONFLICT BEGINS

THE GREAT WAR: THE CONFLICT BEGINS

INTRODUCTION

As with any ongoing war, it is wise to go back to the beginning – to what started the conflict and who the opposing sides are. For our purposes, the beginning of the conflict takes place in the first book of God's Holy Word, the Bible. In Genesis 3, Adam and Eve directly disobey God by eating of the fruit from the tree of the knowledge of good and evil. In Genesis 3:15, for the first time, we are introduced to the opposing sides and the great prophecy that begins to play itself out through the pages of the Old and New Testament writings.

God is speaking to the serpent in Genesis 3:15 when he says, *And I will put **enmity** (a state of opposition) **between you and the woman, and*** *between your seed and her seed; It will bruise your head, and you will bruise his heel."*

The two opposing sides, as stated in the above verse, are the serpent (and his seed) and the woman (and her seed). **The purpose of the ages centers in the seed of the woman, which leads to Christ** (Ephesians 3:11).

It is not so much *Christ* whom Satan stands against, rather, it is *God's purpose in Him*. As this purpose of God successively unfolds, so does Satan's enmity in opposing it. Since the Fall, mankind has never known what true peace is, and will never know it until this great war reaches its climax, and at long last all enemies are subdued and made Christ's footstool (1 Corinthians 15:25, Hebrews 10:13).

Throughout the pages of Scripture, as the seed of the woman is revealed, the attacks to destroy it by Satan and his seed are recorded. There are many physical manifestations and battles in the Old Testament. In the New Testament the war is still being waged but some of the *rules of engagement* have changed. The following pages will show a record of the history and prophecy of this great war, then the current conditions and how we must be equipped to stand today.

First we'll take a better look at the enemy and what makes him tick because the most dangerous enemy is the one we fail to recognize.

GETTING TO KNOW THE ENEMY

GETTING TO KNOW THE ENEMY

In order to be an effective soldier,

You must *know your enemy*.

NAMES AND ALIASES THAT THE ENEMY GOES BY

Accuser: Revelation 12:10

Angel of light (deception): 2 Corinthians 11:14

Devil: Matthew 4:1-11, John 8:44, 1 Peter 5:8; Revelation 12:9, 20:2

Dragon, great dragon: Revelation 12:9, 20:2

Enemy: Matthew 13:39

God of this world (age): 2 Corinthians 4:4

King of Tyrus: Ezekiel 28:12

Liar, father of lies: John 8:44

Lucifer: Isaiah 14:12

Murderer: John 8:44

Prince of demons: Matthew 12:24, Mark 3:22

Prince of the power of the air: Ephesians 2:2

Prince of this world: John 12:31, 14:30, 16:11

Satan (adversary): 1 Chronicles 21:1, Job 1:6-12, 2:1-7, Romans 16:17-20, 2 Corinthians 11:14, 1 Peter 5:8, Revelation 12:9, 20:2

Serpent, old serpent: Genesis 3, Revelation 12:9; 20:2

Tempter: Matthew 4:3

HISTORY
AND
PROPHECY
OF THE ENEMY

HISTORY AND PROPHECY OF THE ENEMY

- There was war in heaven: Michael and his angels fought against *the dragon* and his angels, and *the dragon* and his angels lost and so lost their place in heaven. (Revelation 12:7-9).

- *Lucifer,* the son of the morning, fell from heaven. He was cut down to the ground and weakened the nations. He said in his heart that he would ascend into heaven. He desired to exalt his throne above the stars of GOD and sit also upon the mount of the congregation, in the sides of the north (the dwelling place of God). He wanted to ascend above the heights of the clouds and be like the Most High. Yet he will be brought down to hell, to the sides of the pit. (Isaiah 14:12-15).

- The **King of Tyrus** refers to Satan, who was once blameless, beautiful, wise and an anointed cherub who held a high position in God's purpose. His heart was proud and lifted up because of his beauty and his wisdom was corrupted for the sake of his splendor. God cast him to the ground and will bring forth a fire to consume him, reducing him to ashes upon the earth and he will never be any more. (Ezekiel 28:12-19).

- The **serpent** was more subtle (wise) than any beast of the field which the LORD God had made. He proceeded to tell three lies (contradictions of what God had said – expounded more on the next page) to Eve (Genesis 3:1-15). The **serpent** beguiled her, and she did eat. (2 Corinthians 11:3). Adam was not deceived, but the woman was. (1 Timothy 2:14). The great prophecy and promise of the Great Conflict was pronounced by God in Genesis 3:15.

- He was a **murderer** from the beginning, and abode not in the truth, because there is no truth in him. When he speaks a lie he speaks of his own: for he is a **liar**, and the **father of it.** (John 8:44).

- False apostles, deceitful workers, transform themselves into the apostles of Christ. And it is no wonder, for **Satan** himself is transformed into an **angel of light.** So it is not surprising if his servants also masquerade as ministers of righteousness; but their end will be according to their works. (2 Corinthians 11:13-15).

- The **devil** that deceived them was cast into the lake of fire and brimstone, where the beast and the false prophet are. (Revelation 20:10).

PAST WARFARE: HISTORICAL RECORDS

PAST WARFARE: HISTORICAL RECORDS

This section, based on Appendix 23 from *The Companion Bible.*

3966 BC: Adam is created

(Genesis 1:26-31, 2:7, 15-25).

GENESIS 3:14-15: THE CONFLICT BEGAN

after the serpent (Satan) deceived Eve into eating the fruit that God told Adam that they should not eat of. Satan accomplished this by placing doubt into the minds of Adam & Eve, in the form of three lies.

1. The **first lie** (Genesis 3:1) was to get them to question what God had told them. Opposition to God's Word is Satan's sphere of activity.

2. The **second lie** (Genesis 3:4) centered around contradicting what God had told them earlier in Genesis 2:17.
3. The **third lie** (Genesis 3:5) appealed to their pride (what led to Satan's *own* downfall, that *"they could be as gods, knowing good and evil"*.

Adam and Eve disobeyed God and the Fall of man occurred. God proclaimed the great promise and prophecy stated in Genesis 3:15, *And I will put enmity (a state of opposition) between you and the woman, and between your seed and her seed; It will bruise your head, and you will bruise his heel."* **The great war between the two seeds begins.** (Romans 16:20, 1 Corinthians 15:24-28, Isaiah 53:10-11.)

GENESIS 4:8: ATTACK BY CAIN UPON ABEL

The first murder recorded is between the first two brothers.

The enmity between Cain and Abel that led to the murder was in regard to the acceptance of the offerings that each brought to God. 1 John 3:12 lets us know that Cain was of *that wicked one, and killed his brother because his own works were evil, and his brother's righteous.*

3836 BC: Seth is born

Seth was then appointed as a substitute for Abel so the seed of the woman could continue (Genesis 4:25). The line of Cain is given in Genesis 4:16-24, a line containing names identical in some cases, and similar in others, to names that are found in the true line through Seth, **an indication and a warning, that deception and misdirection are strategies and methods adopted by the enemy to divert the testimony of the Scriptures away from the true seed and purpose to the false.**

GENESIS 6: THE EARTH IS CORRUPTED BY THE 'SONS OF GOD'

Satan strove to corrupt all of mankind. When men began to increase in number on the earth and daughters were born to them, the *sons of God* (refers to fallen angels), saw that the daughters of men were beautiful. The *Nephilim* or giants were the product of the union of the *sons of God* with the daughters of men. The earth became corrupt in the sight of God and was filled with violence. God saw how corrupt the earth had become because all the people on earth had corrupted their ways (Genesis 6:11-12). **Because of this, they had to be destroyed.** There was only one family that was uncontaminated. It was **God who stepped in** to save the race and preserve mankind from a total overthrow.

2910 BC: Noah is born

GENESIS 7:1-3: THE ARK WAS PREPARED AT GOD'S COMMAND

for the express purpose of **keeping the seed of the woman alive on the face of the earth. This was the one and only object of the flood.** *"Noah was a just man and perfect in his* *generations, and Noah walked with God"* (Genesis 6:9). God said to Noah, *"The end of all flesh has come before Me; for the earth is filled with violence through them; and behold, I will destroy them with the earth"* (Genesis 6:13).

2408 BC: Shem is born

GENESIS 9:18-29: AFTER THE FLOOD

(around 2309 BC) the waters subsided, Noah planted a vineyard and drank of the wine, got drunk and laid naked in his tent. His son Ham saw that his father was naked and told his brothers (Leviticus 18:8).

Shem and Japheth took a garment and laid it upon both their shoulders, and went backward, and covered the nakedness of their father so they did not see him naked. When Noah awoke from his wine stupor, he knew what his younger son Ham had done to him and said, **"Cursed be Canaan..."** Canaan was to be one of Ham's sons (Genesis 9:18). **God blessed Shem** (this is the line which eventually Abram would come from) and his line and said He would enlarge Japheth's line.

1951 BC: Abram is born

GENESIS 12:1-3: THE LINE OF SHEM CONTINUES THROUGH ABRAM

when the Lord told Abram to get out of his country and from his kindred and from his father's house, to a land that He would show him. The Lord told him that *"I will make of you a great nation; and I will bless you and make your name great, and you will be a blessing. And I will bless those that bless you and curse those that curse you: and in you will all families of the earth be blessed."* As soon as it was made known that the seed of the woman was to come through Abram there was another irruption of fallen angels (*Nephilim*). Genesis 6:4 says that there were giants (*Nephilim*) not only in those days *before* the Flood, but *after* that as well (See the next section, along with Genesis 13:7, 14:5, 15:18-21, Exodus 23:23, Deuteronomy 7:1-4, 20:17, Numbers 13:32-33, Joshua 12:8).

Continuing, from the call of Abram, Satan's opposition and effort to destroy the seed of the woman will become apparent.

The strategy and aim of the enemy was to occupy Canaan in advance of Abram and so contest its occupation by *his* seed.

It was for the destruction of these (after the days of Noah, more than 500 years after the first irruption), that the *sword of Israel was necessary*, as the purpose of the Flood had been before.

GENESIS 12:10-20: SATAN'S ATTEMPT TO DESTROY ABRAM'S SEED, THROUGH SARAI.

Abram comes to the Land of Canaan where there is an *evil seed*, the Canaanites, Nephilim, the Giants, the sons of Anak and the Rephaim. It is certain that the second irruption took place before Genesis 14 for there the *Rephaim* were mixed up with the five nations or peoples, which included Sodom and Gomorrah, and were defeated by the four kings under Chedorlaomer. When Abram entered Canaan, we read in Genesis 12:6, *"The Canaanite was then* (already) *in the land"*.

In the same chapter, Genesis 12:10-20, we see **SATAN'S NEXT ATTEMPT** was to interfere with Abram's seed (and frustrate the purpose of God that it continue with Isaac). **The enemy used fear and temptation as his strategy.**

There was a famine in the land so Abram travelled south to Egypt with his wife Sarai and his brother's son, Lot. Fear overtook Abram as he thought he might be killed when the Egyptians saw Sarai, (because of her beauty) and found out that she was married to him, so he was tempted to tell them that she was his sister instead so his life would be spared. Sarai *did* come to the attention of Pharaoh just as Abram had feared and was taken into his palace. He treated Abram well for her sake and gave Abram many gifts from livestock to servants.

As through the course of this great conflict, when man fails, **GOD STEPS IN** *so His will and plan will prevail.* This time, instead of a flood, God inflicted serious diseases on Pharaoh and his household because of Sarai (Genesis 12:17) and Pharaoh released Sarai and sent Abram on his way. Abram's seed, through Sarai, was preserved.

This type of attempt was repeated in Genesis 20:1-18, but the Lord intervened ahead of time to warn Abimelech in a dream.

GENESIS 13:7: THE EVIL SEED GROWS

There was strife between the herdsmen of Abram's cattle and Lot's cattle (Genesis 13:7). In Genesis 14:5, *The Nephilim was already known as Rephaim, and Emim* (Deuteronomy 2:10-11) and had established themselves at Ashteroth Karnaim and Shaveh Kiriathaim. In Genesis 15:18-21, the evil seed grows through the different tribes of the Canaanite people: Kenites, Kenizzites, Kadmonites, Hittites, Perizzites, Rephaims, Amorites, Girgashites, and the Jebusites (Genesis 15:19-21, Exodus 3:8 17, 23:23, Deuteronomy 2:20-21, Joshua 3:10).

GENESIS 15: GOD ESTABLISHES HIS COVENANT WITH ABRAM

"To your descendants I give this land, from the river of Egypt to the great river Euphrates – the land of the Kenites, Kenizzites, Kadmonites, Hittites, Perizzites, Rephaims, Amorites, Canaanites, Girgashites and Jebusites."

These people were to be cut off, driven out and utterly destroyed (Deuteronomy 20:17, Joshua 3:10). But Israel failed in this (Joshua 13:13, 15-18, Judges 1:19-20, 28-36, 2:1-5, 3:1-7) and we don't know how many got away to other countries to escape the general destruction. If this was recognized it would go far to solve many problems connected with Anthropology; (see below).

SOMETHING TO THINK ABOUT

If these Nephilim and their branch of Rephaim were associated with Egypt, (Numbers 13:22), we have an explanation of the problem which for ages perplexed all engineers, as to how those huge stones and monuments were brought together. Were they not in Egypt as well as in the *"giant cities of Bashan"*? They were the mighty *"men of renown"*, the explanation of the origin of Greek mythology.

That mythology was no mere invention of human brain, but it grew out of the traditions, memories and legends of the doings of that mighty race of beings; and was gradually evolved out of the *"heroes"* of Genesis 6:4. The fact that they were supernatural in their origin formed an easy step to their being regarded as the demi-gods of the Greeks; hence the Babylonian *"Creation Tablets"*, the Egyptian *"Book of the Dead"*, Greek mythology, and heathen Cosmogonies, which, by some, are set on an equality with the Scripture.

All the corruption and perversion of primitive truths were distorted as their origin was forgotten, and their memories faded away. (Reference *The Companion Bible*, Appendix 25.)

GENESIS 16: ABRAM HAS A SON WITH HAGAR

Through **fear** of not being able to have a child at an old age, Abram falls into **temptation** and listens to his wife Sarai by having a child (Ishmael) with Sarai's maidservant Hagar.

1851 BC: Isaac is born

GENESIS 21:12: ISHMAEL SET ASIDE, ISAAC CHOSEN

"For in Isaac will your seed be called". Ishmael is set aside, but God said to Abraham, *"And also of the son of the bondwoman (Hagar) will I make a nation, because he is thy seed"* (Genesis 21:13).

In addition, regarding Ishmael, Genesis 16:12 says, *"And he will be a wild man; his hand will be against every man, and every man's hand against him; and he will dwell in the presence of all his brethren"*. This is true of the Arab nation today and for over 3,000 years (Genesis 21:20, 2

Chronicles 21:16-17, 22:1, Jeremiah 3:2). In Genesis 24:3, Abraham makes the eldest servant swear by God that he will not allow allow his son, Isaac, to take a wife from the *'daughters of the Canaanites'*. Isaac chooses Rebekah as his wife (Genesis 25:20).

1791 B.C. Esau and Jacob are born

GENESIS 25:23: ESAU AND JACOB BORN

The Lord, speaking to Rebekah says, *Two nations are in your womb, and two manner of people will be separated from your bowels; and one of the people will be stronger than the other people; and the elder will serve the younger."*

GENESIS 26:4: GOD CONTINUES HIS PROMISE TO ABRAHAM THROUGH ISAAC

"And I will make your seed to multiply as the stars of heaven, and will give unto your seed all

these countries; and in your seed shall all the nations of the earth be blessed."

GENESIS 26:34-35: ESAU TAKES HITTITE WIFE, JUDITH

(of Canaanite descent.) For complete genealogy of Esau see Genesis 36.

GENESIS 27: ESAU IS SET ASIDE, JACOB IS CHOSEN

(Genesis 27:9, 28:1, 13-15). **Fear** of famine (Genesis 26:1) allowed Esau to be **tempted** for a bowl of food in exchange for his birthright. *"Esau despised his birthright"* (Genesis 25:29-34). Esau is called a *'profane person'* in Hebrews 12:16.

GENESIS 49:8-12: JUDAH IS CHOSEN

GENESIS 50:20: SATAN'S ATTEMPT TO DESTROY THE CHOSEN FAMILY BY FAMINE BACKFIRES

and is used to save them (referring to Joseph's position in Egypt), attesting to the truth of Proverbs 16:4 and Romans 8:28, *"And we know that all things work together for good to them that love God, to them that are called according to his purpose."*

EXODUS 1:22: SATAN TRIES TO DESTROY THE MALE LINE ALTOGETHER

The next great attempt and object of the enemy of God was to destroy the male line altogether, and so make the birth of *"the seed of the woman"* impossible. In Exodus 1, Satan uses Pharaoh, whose object was to prevent the increase of the Israelites, so that they might not get up out of Egypt, by destroying the male children of Israel at their birth (Exodus 1:10).

GOD AGAIN STEPS IN

to defeat Satan's plan. It is written, *"He takes the wise in their own craftiness"* (Job 5:13) and did so with Pharaoh's *"wisdom"* (Exodus 1:10) by frustrating it with a baby's (Moses) tear (Exodus 2:6).

When Pharaoh's daughter opened the ark of bulrushes, *"she saw the child, and behold the babe wept. And she had compassion on him."* So Pharaoh's "wisdom" ended up bringing up the very man (Moses) that helped lead the Israelites out of captivity (Exodus 14:30-31, Hebrews 11:23, 28-29).

JUDGES 4-5

Jabin (king of Canaan) is used by the enemy to abduct the women in Israel. The true motive was revealed in Judges 5:30 through Sisera's (captain of Jabin's army) mother when she wonders where they are and why they haven't divided the prey (the damsels or maidens) that they were fighting for so they each could have a maiden or two per warrior. Deborah sang *"until I Deborah arose"*, who was called of God to deliver the women of Israel, and so become a mother indeed (Judges 5:7).

1040 BC: David is born

1 SAMUEL 16:1, 12-13: THE PROMISE IS MADE CONCERNING DAVID.

Saul's javelin was used to attempt his destruction (1 Samuel 18:10-11). *"Saul became David's enemy continually"* (1 Samuel 18:29).

2 SAMUEL 7:16: THE PROPHECY CONCERNING DAVID'S REIGN & THRONE

"And your house and your kingdom will be established for ever before you: your throne will be established for ever." After David's line was singled out (2 Samuel 7:5-16), it was the next selected for assault.

NOTE
While the successor to the throne came through Solomon (Matthew 1:1-6,16), Mary's line (the seed of the woman) descends through Nathan, Solomon's brother (Luke 3:31), and so has

special reference to the king and kingdom (Luke 1:31-33).

847-839 BC

2 CHRONICLES 21-22: THE ENEMY TRIES TO BREAK UP THE ROYAL LINE BY WHICH THE SEED WAS TO COME

On the death of Jehoshaphat, his son Jehoram *"slew all his brothers with the sword"* (2 Chronicles 21:4). So the Royal line was reduced to himself – one life. But he had children and of these, we read the the Arabians came up against Judah, and slew all his sons, *"so that there was not a son left to him, except Ahaziah,* (also known as Jehoahaz) *the youngest of his sons"* (2 Chronicles 21:16-17, 22:1).

When Ahaziah died, Athaliah killed *"all the Seed royal"* (2 Chronicles 22:10). The babe Joash alone was rescued; and, for six years, **the faithfulness of Jehovah's word** was at stake (2 Chronicles 22:11-12, 23:3).

483-473 BC

ESTHER 3:6, 12-13; 6:1: ANOTHER FULL FRONTAL ATTACK ON THE WHOLE NATION

"The adversary and enemy is this wicked Haman" (Esther 7:6). While Israel was in captivity in Persia, Haman was used to attempt the destruction of the whole nation.

A *"small thing"* (**AS GOD STEPPED IN**) was used to frustrate the design of "the Jew's enemy". A sleepless night; that was all but enough as the king found out the truth when he read the book of records/chronicles when he couldn't sleep (Esther 6:1-3). Satan's plans were once again defeated.

Satan, not easily discouraged, stood before the woman ready to devour her child as soon as it should be born.

THE HOUR CAME WHEN THE SEED OF THE WOMAN ENTERED INTO THE WORLD (John 1:14, Romans 1:3, 2 Timothy 2:8; Galatians 3:16, Revelation 12:17).

FOR THE LINEAGE OF JESUS CHRIST REFER TO

Matthew 1:1-16, Luke 3:23-38.

Jesus is conceived
(John 1:14; Luke 1:31).

MATTHEW 2:3-8, 16: HEROD IS USED TO DESTROY THE CHILD

When Herod had found out the place (Bethlehem) from the Scribes (Matthew 2:4-5) and the time when the star appeared from the wise men (Matthew 2:7), he had all the babes (under the age of 2 yrs. old) in Bethlehem slain and thought he had devoured the seed of the woman. But again **God stepped in** and defeated his plans by warning Joseph in a dream to flee with his wife and child to Egypt until Herod was dead (Matthew 2:13, 19-21).

29 AD: Jesus ministry begins

MATTHEW 4:1-10: SATAN ATTACKS THROUGH FEAR AND TEMPTATION.

The suggestion by Satan that Christ should throw himself down from the pinnacle of the Temple (Matthew 4:6); the attempt of the people of Nazareth to cast him down from the brow of the hill (Luke 4:29); the two storms on the Lake (Matthew 8:24, Mark 4:37, Luke 8:23), were all so many foiled attempts of Satan to devour the seed of the woman, Jesus Christ.

33 AD: Jesus death and resurrection

When Satan saw Jesus on the cross, laid in the tomb, and the stone sealed, he thought he had achieved victory but again almighty **GOD STEPPED IN**, raising him from the dead. Christ is presently seated and waiting (Hebrews 10:12-

13), hidden in the house of God on high (Revelation 3:21); and the members of *"the one body"* are hidden there *"in Him"* (Colossians 3:1-3). The enemy over-reached himself in the death of Christ for in that lay the purpose of God eventually *"by death to destroy him who has the power of death"* (Hebrews 2:14).

THE PARABLE OF THE WEEDS (TARES)

THE PARABLE OF THE WEEDS (TARES)

Matthew 13:24-30, 36-43

(New International Version)

Jesus told them another parable:

"The kingdom of heaven is like a man who sowed good seed in his field. But while everyone was sleeping, his enemy came and sowed weeds among the wheat, and went away. When the wheat sprouted and formed heads (ears), then the weeds also appeared. The owner's servants came to him and said, 'Sir, don't you sow good seed in your field? Where then did the weeds come from?' '**An Enemy Did This,**' he replied. The servants asked him, 'Do you want us to go and pull them up?' 'No,' he answered, 'because while you are pulling the weeds, you may root up the wheat with them. **Let both grow together until the harvest.** At that time I will tell the harvesters: First collect the weeds and tie them in bundles to be burned; then gather the wheat and bring it into my barn." Then he left the crowd and went into the house. His disciples came to him and said "Explain to us the parable of the weeds in the field." He answered, **"The one who sowed the good seed is the Son of Man. The field is the world,** and **the good seed stands for the sons of the kingdom. The weeds are the sons of the evil one, and the enemy who sows them is the devil.** The harvest is the end of the age, and the harvesters are angels. "As the weeds are pulled up and burned in the fire, so it will be at the end of the age. The Son of Man will send out his angels, and they will weed out of his kingdom everything that causes sin and all who do evil. They will throw them into the fiery furnace, where there will be weeping and gnashing of teeth. Then the righteous will shine like the sun in the kingdom of their Father. He who has ears, let him hear."

As we have seen, the **Enemy's Tactics and Plans Involve Trickery and Deceit** – taking something true and Godly and perverting it ever so slightly to deceive and bring into captivity as many as possible. Tares (zizania), while growing, look like wheat, but when full grown the ears are long and the grains almost black. Each grain of zewan (zizanion) must be removed before grinding wheat or the bread is bitter and poisonous. Wheat is golden; but tares show their true color as they ripen.

The reason for the delay in the setting up of the kingdom is discovered in the fact that **an enemy is at work.** Side by side with the true children of the kingdom are the children of the wicked one, but these are not removed until the end of the age. Be careful and prayerful, the offspring of Satan are often so morally perfect as to be indistinguishable from true believers – the good seed. Yet they are the seed of the serpent. Today, through the media: movies, music, internet; schools, churches, families…*wherever you are,* **the tares are with the wheat**-side by side-**hard to tell apart.**

PRESENT
WARFARE

PRESENT WARFARE

OUR CALL OF DUTY TODAY

After the final rejection of Christ by the Jewish Dispersion, in Rome (fulfillment of the prophecy of Isaiah 6:9-10), Paul proclaimed that the salvation of God has been sent to the Gentiles (nations), and that they will hear it (Acts 28:25-28.)

So for those today who have put their trust in the Lord Jesus Christ, after hearing the gospel of their salvation, and believe, have been sealed with the Holy Spirit of promise (Ephesians 1:12-13).

Our enemy, Satan, did not cease fire in the war when Christ ascended into heaven. He just regrouped his troops and began battling in a new sphere (arena), but essentially with the same aim. He is still at work trying to carry out the same opposition (enmity), but this time, by doing all he can to prevent or hinder God's purposes in Christ (through us) from being accomplished.

Even though there will not be a total peace or cease-fire in the world until the Beast is taken, the Anti-Christ destroyed, and Satan bound, God has provided all we need to equip ourselves, as soldiers in Christ, to stand against the wiles (methods) of our enemy today. 2 Corinthians 10:3-4 reminds us that even though we walk in the flesh, we do not war after the flesh: for the weapons of our warfare are not carnal, but mighty through God to the pulling down of strongholds.

The necessary gear that will enable us to stand strong in the power of His might is found in Ephesians 6:10-18.

WE WILL BE COMPLETELY PROTECTED, ONLY WHEN WE ARE WEARING THE COMPLETE ARMOR OF GOD

… because we wrestle *not* against flesh and blood (human beings as opposed to wicked spirits), but against principalities (rulers), against powers (authorities), against the rulers of the darkness (the present order of things) of this world (age), against spiritual wickedness (wicked spirits of the evil one).

EQUIPMENT CHECK LIST

- **Belt of Truth** (to counter-attack the false)

- **Breastplate of Righteousness** (Isaiah 11:5, 59:17)
- Preparation of the **gospel of peace** as **footgear**
- **Shield of Faith** (to extinguish all the fiery darts of the wicked)
- **Helmet of Salvation**
- **Sword of the Spirit** (the Word of God)

Thus, *there are six pieces.*

The first three (belt, breastplate, foot gear) are to be put on or worn.

In order for the belt of Truth to function effectively it must be dispensational and rightly divided (2 Timothy 2:15-16). It must be based on sound doctrine (1 Timothy 1:10-11, 2 Timothy 1:13).

Recall some of the aliases of the enemy on pages nine and ten: *Liar, father of lies* and *Angel of light* (deception). It is in the realm of false doctrine (teaching that the wiles (methods) of the devil are to be discovered.

The next two (shield, helmet) are weapons of defense.

These pieces will enable us to stand and withstand the assaults of the enemy. The shield of faith is necessary to put out the fiery darts being thrown our way. Ephesians 4:14 says, "...in order that we may no longer be children tossed to and fro, and carried about with every wind of doctrine (evil teaching of the ruler of the air and of demons), by the sleight (trickery) of men, and cunning craftiness (to the deceit of error). Colossians 2:8 warns us, "Beware so that no one carries you off as spoil (robs you) or makes you captive through philosophy and vain deceit, after the tradition of men, after the rudiments (elements) of the world, and not after Christ."

Remember that the enemy's methods (ways) of sleight and subtle deception have been perfected since the ancient of days. The victims and casualties who fall prey for his tactics do so many times unaware of the lies that they are believing about themselves, the world and God.

They, obviously, forgot to equip themselves with key pieces of gear.

WIELDING THE WORD OF THE SPIRIT

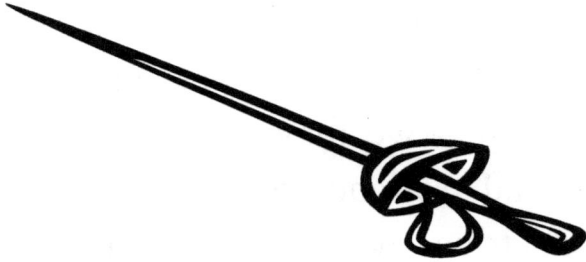

The last piece is the *only* offensive piece.

It is the only piece that will allow us to *wrestle*.

It is the Sword of the Spirit (the Word of God).

THIS IS THE ONLY WEAPON THAT TERRIFIES OUR ENEMY THE DEVIL

… and because of this, becoming familiar with this weapon should become our top and main priority, so that we can be as effective as Christ was with it when he was being tempted in the wilderness (Matthew 4:1-11). The soldier of Christ stands for all the truth of God, against the lie, and in tour of duty and out of tour of duty he should wield the sword of the Spirit by preaching the Word, with boldness and precision (2 Timothy 4:2).

All other weapons which are not found in God's Word are carnal weapons that will not be useful and should be rejected absolutely.

DUTIES AND RESPONSIBILITIES OF A SOLDIER IN CHRIST

A SOLDIER IN CHRIST IS THE FULL-GROWN MAN.

In the Old Testament to be a soldier, bear arms and go to war, you had to be 20 years of age (Numbers 1:3). In the New Testament, Ephesians-sense, the believer that is *not* a babe, but can take in meat (Hebrews 5:12-14) *is* the full-grown man or soldier.

A SOLDIER IN CHRIST PLEASES HIS COMMANDER

"Endure hardness (evil), as a good soldier of Jesus Christ. No man that wars (serves as a soldier) entangles himself with the affairs of this life; so he may please him who has chosen him to be a soldier" (2 Timothy 2:3-4). The chief commander's commendation is the reward.

A SOLDIER IN CHRIST'S CONDUCT IS ABOVE REPROACH

A good soldier flees youthful lusts, follows righteousness, faith, love and peace (with them that call on the Lord out of a pure heart). He avoids foolish and unlearned questions (knowing that they do stir up strife). He does not strive and is gentle to all (apt to teach, patient, in meekness instructs those that oppose him); in the hope that God may grant those that will repent, to come to know the truth and so come to their senses and escape out of the enemy's snare of captivity (2 Timothy 2:22-26).

A good soldier is able to stand by first fleeing from fornication, idolatry (anything that can be placed in the position of God), the love of money, and youthful lusts (1 Corinthians 6:18, 10:14, 1 Timothy 6:11, 2 Timothy 2:22).

When he walks, he walks in love (Ephesians 5:1-2); as a child of light (Ephesians 5:8); and wisely (Ephesians 5:15).

A SOLDIER IN CHRIST IS PREPARED AND ALERT

An effective soldier in Christ is constantly filling, replenishing and thus renewing himself in the Spirit, which is the Word of God (Ephesians 4:23,5:18, 6:17). "Praying always with all prayer and supplication in the Spirit, and watching thereunto with all perseverance and supplication for all saints" (Ephesians 6:18). He does not sleep, as others do, but watches and is sober (1 Thessalonians 5:6), as he puts on the breastplate of faith and love; and the hope of salvation as a helmet (1 Thessalonians 5:8).

A good soldier is sober and vigilant; because his adversary the devil, walks about as a roaring lion, seeking someone he may devour (1 Peter 5:8).

A SOLDIER IN CHRIST KNOWS HIS SECURE POSITION TODAY

He does not wage warfare, attempt to conquer, or fight as they did in Old Testament times (prior to Jesus Christ's coming, death, and resurrection).

He understands that he is now camouflaged or HID with Christ in God where Satan, the enemy, can never come.

As an impenetrable foxhole, covered by the complete armor of God.

The enemy has *no* power over that life which is hid with Christ in God, and the believer is as secure as those who were hidden in the secret place of the Most High (Psalm 91:5-13).

THE LORD KNOWS THOSE WHO ARE HIS

"Everyone who confesses the name of the Lord must turn away from wickedness" (2 Timothy 2:19).

Our Commander in Chief, God says, *"I will never leave you nor forsake you"* (Hebrews 13:5) and because of this, as trusting soldiers, we can boldly say, *"The Lord is my helper,"* and *"I will not fear what man shall do to me"* (Psalm 118:6).

A SOLDIER IN CHRIST KNOWS THE TRAINING MANUAL

His *only* source of truth is his training manual, the living Word of God –and he looks at *everything* in light of it (2 Timothy 3:15-17).

He studies diligently to show and present himself approved to his Commander, God.

He isn't ashamed, as he rightly divides the word of truth (2 Timothy 2:15).

A SOLDIER IN CHRIST STAYS CLOSE TO BASE & OUT OF TROUBLE

He does not quarrel about words knowing that it is of no value and only ruins those who listen (2 Timothy 2:14).

He avoids profane and vain babblings (godless chatter), because those who indulge in it will become more and more ungodly (2 Timothy 2:16).

He walks honestly, as in the day, not in rioting and drunkenness, not in chambering (co-habitation) and wantonness (lustful acts), not in strife (fighting) and envying (Romans 13:12-13).

A SOLDIER IN CHRIST UNDERSTANDS HE WILL SUFFER

"All who live godly lives in Christ Jesus will suffer persecution. Evil men and seducers will grow worse and worse as they deceive and are being deceived" (2 Timothy 3:12-13).

"For therefore we both labor and suffer reproach, because we trust in the living God, who is the Savior of all men, specially of those that believe" (1 Timothy 4:10).

COMMUNICATION PLAN AND FOCUS

A soldier in Christ realizes that the war is within his old nature (the flesh), the sin dwelling in him (Romans 7:18-25). The enemy (like the Canaanites in the Old Testament) has already occupied the land (the old nature) in advance. He set up camp and has been residing in it since the fall of mankind (Romans 3:23, 1 Corinthians 15:22). The command has gone out that the soldier is not to have anything to do with his old nature. He is to give it no attention. In his commander, God's sight, it was crucified when Christ was crucified and he is to *'reckon it as dead'* (Romans 6:11). He is to put on the Lord Jesus Christ, and make no provision for the flesh, to fulfill the lusts of it (Romans 13:14).

"Greater is He that is in you,
than he that is in the world" (1 John 4:4).

THERE IS TO BE NO COMMUNICATION WITH WHAT IS DEAD

The soldier's course is clear. He is to separate; and go *"outside the camp"* (Hebrews 13:13) altogether. The word 'camp' is the same word that is translated 'armies' in Hebrews 11:34. The soldier should not form another camp of his own among their camps, but go forth 'to Him", the Commander, Who has gone into the holiest of all even Heaven itself. That is now his place of worship and His Commander, God is his one object of worship.

FOCUS ABOVE

The focus is to be on the Giver, not on the soldier or anywhere else. The focus is to be on the Blesser, who is the faithful and trustworthy steward of *all* blessings.

"Let us look to Jesus the Author and Finisher of our faith, Who for the joy that was set before Him endured the cross, despising the shame, and is set down at the right hand of the throne of God" (Hebrews 12:2).

****

**"If you then be risen with Christ,
seek those things which are above,
where Christ sits on the right hand of God.
Set your affection on things above,
not on things on the earth.
For you are dead,
and your life is hid with Christ in God.
When Christ, Who is our life, shall appear,
then you will also appear with Him in glory."
(Colossians 3:1-4)**

EPILOGUE: SATAN, THE ENEMY, IS A DEFEATED FOE!

EPILOGUE: SATAN, THE ENEMY, IS A DEFEATED FOE!

"And the devil that deceived them was cast into the lake of fire and brimstone, where the beast and the false prophet (are)."
(Revelation 20:10)

"There shall be no more death, neither sorrow, nor crying, neither shall there be any more pain: for the former things are passed away."
(Revelation 21:4)

"And there will be no more curse: but the throne of God and of the Lamb will be in it…"
(Revelation 22:3)

"The last enemy that shall be destroyed is death."
(1 Corinthians 15:26)

"When all things shall be subdued (subjected) to
Him,
then will the son also Himself be subject to Him
that put all things under Him,
that God may be all in all
(everywhere supreme, all things in all places)."
(1 Corinthians 15:28)

TERMS
TO KNOW

TERMS TO KNOW

American Dictionary of the English Language:
Noah Webster 1828

Arms: Weapons of offense, or armor for defense and protection of the body.

Battle: A fight, or encounter between enemies, or opposing armies; an engagement.

Captives: A prisoner taken by force or stratagem in war, by an enemy.

Conflict: A striking or dashing against each other as of two moving bodies in opposition, violent collision of substance.

Enemy: A foe; an adversary; one who hates or dislikes; an enemy to truth or falsehood.

Enmity: The quality of being an enemy; the opposite of friendship; ill will; hatred; unfriendly disposition; malevolence.

Soldier: A man engaged in military service; one whose occupation is military; a brave warrior.

Stratagem: A plan or scheme for deceiving an enemy.

Tactics: Everything that relates to the order, formation and disposition of armies and their encampments.

War: A contest; state of hostility, opposition

Warfare: Contest; struggle with spiritual enemies.

Weapons: Anything used or designed to be used in destroying or annoying an enemy.

MORE ON SATAN

MORE ON SATAN

Satan through the Bible
By Sylvia Penny

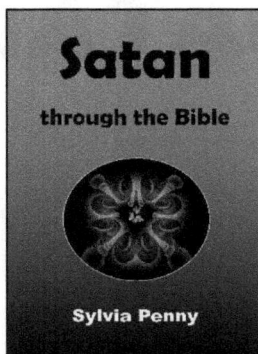

This is a comprehensive treatment of all that the Bible has to say about Satan. Starting with his creation before Eden, it follows him and his activities throughout the Bible, culminating with his demise in the lake of fire.

It considers many of his different names and titles, dealing with what they mean or signify. It discusses such issues as whether or not Satan is omnipresent, and just how much he knows and understands.

And we have details and explanations about every encounter Satan had with people including Eve and Job, Jesus and Judas, Peter and Paul, and many others.

We have a great and powerful enemy, and it is important that we have a Biblical view of who he is, what he is like, and how he can influence both individuals and society today.

****

More details of the above book can be seen on

www.obt.org.uk

It can be ordered from that website and also from The Open Bible trust, Fordland Mount, Upper Basildon, Reading, RG8 8LU, UK.

It is also available as an eBook from Amazon and Apple and also as a KDP paperback from Amazon.

ABOUT THE AUTHOR

Laura Kestly was born in Dubuque, Iowa, USA, in 1962 and raised in Racine, Wisconsin. She received her Bachelor of Fine Arts degree in 1985. Laura served for three years on a Christian school board, chairing the education and curriculum committees. She teaches Sunday school at *Open Bible Fellowship* and is a freelance artist and writer. She has written the monthly newsletter *Just a Moment,* for the past 12 years, which can be accessed on her website: www.cagedbirdsings.org. Laura lives with her husband, two sons, and English bulldog west of Milwaukee, Wisconsin.

ABOUT THIS BOOK

WAR MANUAL

As with any ongoing war, it is wise to go back to the beginning— to what started the conflict and who the opposing sides are.

We first read of the conflict of the ages in Genesis 3. There we are introduced to the opposing sides—God and Satan … and from then on Adam and Eve, and all who followed, including us, are caught in the middle.

What can we do about it?

****

Publications of The Open Bible Trust must be in accordance with its evangelical, fundamental and dispensational basis. However, beyond this minimum, writers are free to express whatever beliefs they may have as their own understanding, provided that the aim in so doing is to further the object of The Open Bible Trust. A copy of the doctrinal basis is available on **www.obt.org.uk** or from:

THE OPEN BIBLE TRUST
Fordland Mount, Upper Basildon,
Reading, RG8 8LU, UK.

www.ingramcontent.com/pod-product-compliance
Lightning Source LLC
Chambersburg PA
CBHW070555030426
42337CB00016B/2505